# Don't Take My Grief Away From Me

# Don't Take My Grief Away From Me

## How to Walk Through Grief and Learn to Live Again

### *Third Edition*

In-Sight Books, Inc
Oklahoma City

# Don't Take My Grief Away From Me
## How to Walk Through Grief and Learn to Live Again
### Doug Manning

Third Edition ©2011

In-Sight Books, Inc
PO Box 42467
Oklahoma City, Oklahoma 73123
800.658.9262 or 405.810.9501
www.InSightBooks.com
OrdersAndInfo@InSightBooks.com

First Edition ©1979 by In-Sight Books, Inc.
Second Edition ©2005 by In-Sight Books, Inc.

*Printed in the United States of America*

ISBN-10: 1-892785-74-9
ISBN-13: 978-1-892785-74-9

In-Sight Books, Inc.
Since 1979  Grief & Elder Care Resources

11/12

## Dedication

To Ann and Jess Wade—
   The night of their great loss gave birth to this book.
This book is dedicated to them in the hope that their
honesty in grief can produce healing for all who read it.

*March 1, 1979*

# Preface

*Don't Take My Grief Away From Me* was published in 1979 as Doug Manning's first venture into offering comforting words, heartfelt understanding, and encouraging guideposts for people on the grief journey. It began his career as an author and speaker in the areas of grief and elder care and was the cornerstone of his company, In-Sight Books, Inc. Millions of copies have been sold all over the world in the past thirty-two years. Doug often said he would like to revisit the book and add some of the lessons learned in his years of walking with hurting individuals but just did not know how to revise a book that had worked for so many for so many years.

On September 25, 2010, Doug's wife of fifty-seven years died and his world was significantly changed. He decided that it was time—time to update and expand this most beloved book. It was time to share some of the personal experiences and wisdom gained on his own path to healing, as well as offering stories of struggle and promise from some of the thousands of individuals who have shared their hearts with him. The title remains the same because that phrase is the foundation of all of Doug's work; people need permission and safety to grieve without it being taken away from them.

Doug's hope is that this new edition will provide fresh perspectives, gems of truth, and honest discussions about the universal experience of grief. This is his gift for anyone who shares these pages hoping to understand how to survive the pain of loss and how to ultimately find moments of gratitude and peace on their own grief journey.

# For Barbara
## 1934-2010

The doctor said she was gone
A few moments before
while they worked frantically to bring her back
he had said it was time for her to go
and asked me to allow her to do so
now he simply said
she is gone.

He was wrong
She is not here in person
and I cannot touch her
or hold her in my arms
and I know the loneliness of a house too large
with too much space to echo
the hollow sounds of silence
back to me.
But she is not gone.

The months have passed
and I have stopped waiting to hear her
come home from work
and the sound of her unique little shuffle
as she walked through the house
and no longer look at the bed every morning
to see if she is awake yet.
But she is not gone.

No one is dead until they are forgotten
And we will never forget
So she will live on
In the lives she touched
As Mother
Grandmother
Great Grandmother
Wife and friend
No way for her to be gone

*Every day we laugh at some memory*
*Of how frugal she was*
*An eraser held together by tape*
*More note pads than the printer*
*And almost as may pens as Staples*
*Her desk has become a shrine to remind us*
*How quietly she served us and never*
*Called it a job.*
*She is not gone you know.*

*We cry through holidays*
*Wishing she were here*
*But so grateful that she was*
*And that she loved us with no reservation*
*And no judgment*
*And take pictures in her honor*
*While wondering what to do with the thousands she took.*
*She is still here.*

*She lives on in life beyond life*
*Whatever and wherever that is*
*It is a better place because she is there*
*And we hope*
*Someone makes her laugh every day*
*And her feet and hands feel no more pain*
*And that they have cameras there*
*So she can take pictures and*
*Plan to put them in albums*

*But mostly she lives here*
*In the stories we will never stop telling*
*The memories we will never stop sharing*
*The life we will never stop honoring*
*And the person we will never stop loving*
*She is not dead*
*She just moved to the inside of our hearts.*

# Contents

*If I could do what I wanted to do for you right now,*
*I would make you feel normal.*
*I would hold your hand as you told me of the feelings*
*you are having inside, and I would say—*
*Yes, that is how it feels to be in grief.*
*Yes, that is a normal reaction.*
*Yes, as you progress through grief you*
*have thoughts like that.*

*I cannot be there to hold your hand and say yes.*
*I hope this book will be a substitute—*
*I hope it will let you know you are normal.*

*Grief is bad enough. To experience it and not know what*
*to expect or how you should feel makes the experience*
*worse—much worse.*

*Read on and learn to feel normal.*

*Grieving is as natural as crying
when you are hurt, sleeping
when you are tired,
eating when you are hungry, or
sneezing when your nose itches.
It is nature's way of healing a
broken heart.*

# Chapter 1

# Don't Take My Grief Away From Me

I have always thought she was brilliance under pressure. Her statement was a flash of insight in a time of darkness—a flash of insight which ultimately changed my career and my life.

Her little girl had the croup. Nothing seemed serious or unusual about it. Eighteen-month-old children can be sick enough to scare parents to death and two hours later they seem totally well. The croup worsened and the child was admitted to the hospital. Still there was no cause for fear. An oxygen tent, a vaporizer, some antibiotics and all would be well. The husband went home to care for the other child. In thirty minutes the child was dead. Just dead. This beautiful, effervescent life was gone.

Of all times for me to be 700 miles away on vacation, I had to pick this time. These were members of the church where I was serving as pastor and were also dear friends. In their hour of deepest need, I was away. As little as I knew about grief then, I probably would not have been much help had I been there. I would have felt better, but I am not sure this couple would have been helped very much by my presence or my philosophical answers.

The young mother was crying hysterically. It is strange that we cannot allow tears. Nothing is more natural than to cry. Nothing gets as quick a reaction from us as someone crying out of control. Everyone there that night began to react:

"There, there—now get hold of yourself."

"You can't carry on like this."

"Come on now—stop crying."

Suddenly she stopped, stepped back, looked at them and said, "Don't take my grief from me. I deserve it. I am going to have it."

I did not hear her make the statement, and yet her words have haunted me for years. Her words have also done more to change my concept of grief and the needs of grieving people than any words I have ever heard.

I wondered how many times I had tried to take grief away from folks. How many times I had denied them the right to grieve in my presence because it was evident that I was not comfortable with pain or tears.

I wondered how many times I had filled the air with philosophical statements designed to reassure me and to explain away tragedy far more than they were designed to help the person in grief.

I wondered how many times I had succumbed to the idea that sympathy was somehow harmful. It was almost as if I believed that if sympathy were given, people would wallow in it and never get well. These feelings seemed to be my stance.

I wondered how many times I had taken away grief by sheer neglect. When the funeral was over, my work was done. I might have been a little more attentive the next time the person came to church; beyond that, I went on as if nothing had happened. Most of the time they appeared to go on as if nothing had happened, while inside they wept.

I wondered how many times I had taken away a person's grief by my efforts to avoid the intimacy and feelings I was forced to face in the process.

A young minister and his wife lost a child in a car wreck. They had many friends closer to them than my wife and me, yet they seemed drawn to our house. They came by night after night. When I dropped by their house they seemed relieved and pleased. One night they told us the reason. We were the only ones willing to talk about their child. We called her by name and seemed to be comfortable in doing so. Everyone else seemed to take great pains in avoiding the subject. If the child was mentioned, the subject was changed abruptly. When they told us we were different I breathed a sigh of relief. I had stopped trying to take away grief and had begun helping people walk through it.

These experiences created so much interest in me that I started a study of grief that is still going on today. I read the few books that were available at that time and started a grief group long before they were in vogue. My passion about grief changed my life and my career. The goal of my life is to give people the freedom and the permission to grieve without someone trying to take it away.

People will try to take grief away from you also. They will not intend to, nor even realize they are doing so. You may not realize this is being done to you, but the effort will be there. The effort is subtle but very effective.

# The Pattern

There seems to be a set pattern built within us that becomes our automatic reaction to grief or pain. As soon as someone shares their situation we seem to react in three progressive ways.

**First We Explain:**

After years of counseling and writing, I still have to catch myself. When someone tells me their story I want to begin explaining either why this happened or how they should feel about what happened. You may have already been bombarded with explanations. People do this because they do not know what to say and they want to make you feel better. They have no idea how foolish the explanations sound and how much anger they create.

Most of the explanations are designed to defend God, as if He needs our defense or as if we actually know how the universe works. The explanations usually start with, "Perhaps this happened because..." The young minister whose child was killed in a car crash was told, "Perhaps your child would have grown up to be a bad person and God took her home before that could happen." As horrific as that sounds, the person who said that was not an uncaring person. He was trying to help, but he saw help as explanation.

You have the right and the obligation to ask why. To question and express anger is not just a right, it is part of the healing process. But the bottom line is there really are no answers or adequate explanations to why bad things happen to us.

One of my favorite stories tells of a young student who fell asleep in seminary class. The professor stares at him until he awakens with a start. The professor said, "Young man tell us why is there evil and suffering in the world?" The student stammered for a moment and then said, "I used to know the answer to that question but I forgot it." The professor said, "Mark this day well, for in the history of man there have only been two people who knew the answer to that question. One was Jesus Christ and He didn't tell us, and the other was this young man, and he forgot."

The explanations are efforts to relieve your grief, but they actually tend to trivialize it, and trivialization leaves a person feeling like no one understands how deep they hurt. They end up feeling alone with no one to walk beside them while they face the long journey of grief.

**If Explanations Don't Work, Then Comes the Arguing:** You may begin to hear: "Now you can't let yourself feel that way," "That is not how you should see this loss," "This is certainly bad, but think of how much worse it could have been," or "You know your loved one is better off and that should make you feel better." The last part of that is implied rather than stated. Believe me, you will get plenty of implications in the days ahead.

Again, these people are trying to help, but they really think that changing the way you think will automatically change the way you feel. If you will just see it differently you will feel better. They do not understand that feelings do not always follow thoughts. Understanding the whys and how of something does not always match how we feel or respond.

**If Explanations and Arguments Do Not Work,
Then They Begin to Criticize:**
I hope you never hear "You are not trying to get well, you are just wallowing in your grief." It is amazing how much those who have never been there know what grief is like and what you need. Almost everyone who goes through a loss has to, at some time, deal with those who think they know and, unfortunately, feel the need to tell.

All of these are efforts to take your grief away. None will work or even help. Grief is a journey to be walked, not a situation to be explained, nor a pattern to be followed. The answer is to understand the process and find the strength and the freedom to walk the path in your own unique way.

*Grief* is not a walk in the park,
but it certainly is a strange
and sometimes
scary journey

## Chapter 2

# The Journey No One Wants to Take

I referred to grief being a "journey" in an article and immediately got a response from a woman who said, "If you think grief is just a walk in the park you are wrong." I have no idea how she decided that was what I was saying. The article certainly did not indicate that idea in any way, but I learned long ago that there is no way to predict how we will respond when we are grieving. Suddenly words we never noticed can become words to argue about. Grief is not a walk in the park, but it certainly is a strange and sometimes scary journey through pain and feelings we never thought we would experience, through reactions we cannot begin to explain and angers that seem strange even to us.

And here you are beginning just that kind of a journey. It is a journey no one wants to take and all of us dread. Right now you must be wondering if you can even survive, much less complete, this journey. The whirl in your mind and the whirl all around you makes it feel like there is not one solid place to stand. Grief is a fearful leap into the unknown. My goal and my hope is to be a companion who walks along with you on your journey.

I do not believe in grief counseling. Counseling is best used for people with mental or emotional problems. I believe in grief *companioning*. You need someone to walk beside you and simply try to understand what you are feeling, even though it is impossible for others to actually comprehend the experience. The fact that they try means more than words can tell. My hope is that this book will be a companion as well. Perhaps I will understand at least some of what you feel and we can walk together.

I wrote this edition of this book several months after the death of my wife of fifty-seven years, so many of my observations and thoughts about grief were challenged or confirmed during my journey. I will refer to my experience only on occasion. This book is not about me. I hope it is all about you and your experience.

There are some little known things about the journey that it might help to know from the start. As you are able to do so, read as many of these first few chapters as you can. I think they will help prepare you for the road ahead.

*Eternity will have to last a
  long time—
I have enough questions to fill
  up a thousand years.*

# Chapter 3

# There Are No Magical Words

There is no such thing as comfort, if by comfort we mean some word or set of words that will somehow make the pain go away. Our society seems to be convinced that explaining why your loved one died or telling you how much better off they are will make it all better. The bottom line to grief is your loved one is not here, and you must learn to live without them being here.

I have a friend who attended a meeting where a woman was supposed to be able to communicate with the dead. My friend's daughter and her husband had both died and she was one of the ones in the audience whose loved ones spoke through the medium. She was, and is, convinced the experience was real. I am far too much of a cynic to be objective on that point and it does not really matter whether or not it was real for our purpose here. The only thing that matters is she thought the experience was real and that she had spoken to both of them. They were together and happy.

She called me the next day and asked to come to my office. She told me about the experience and how real it seemed to be. Then she said:

When the meeting was over people almost mobbed me. They were hugging me and congratulating me saying they knew that must be a very healing experience for me. They even followed me into the restroom to tell me more about how I should be feeling. The reason I am here today is I don't feel any better and cannot understand why I don't. I just talked with my daughter and my husband. I found out they were in a better place, they were together and at peace, and I still feel the same. Why?

I said, "You do not feel better because your daughter and husband are still gone. The bottom line of grief is they are not here and you are trying to learn to live with them not being here. It is wonderful that they are in a better place and at peace. One day that will become a very precious thought for you, but right now knowing that does not put his car in your driveway or her laughter in the house."

Just as there are no magical words that guarantee you will feel better, there are no answers to the always present questions that can actually make the questions go away.

Asking "why" is normal and healthy, and no one should take questioning away from you. Asking "why this happened" or "why me" is a very good way to bleed off some of the frustration and anger. Having someone try to answer the questions by quoting some platitude can be maddening, but, hopefully, that won't stop you from shouting your questions from the housetops as long as you realize that finding an answer is really not the answer.

A woman whose son died in a car accident kept shouting at everyone she met "Why did this happen?

Why won't anyone tell me why? I need to know why God took my son."

I let her ask over and over until she began to calm a little and then said,

> I do not want to keep you from asking the question. You have the right to question and it helps to get the feelings out by doing so. I do not have an answer that is worthy of your question nor do I have one that will automatically make you feel better. If I did have an answer, and if it was so logical and clear you could not deny that it came directly from God, and if the answer cleared your mind so completely that you would never question again, you would still hurt. Your pain does not come from your lack of an answer. Your pain comes from the fact that your son is dead and you must learn to live without his being here.

Answers do not make that pain go away. Unfortunately, most of your friends do not know this. You will probably be facing this issue during your entire journey. Friends and family mean well. They are trying to help, but they see help as explanations and new ways to think.

Some grieving folks have a struggle going to church, at least during the early days of their grief. Sometimes they struggle with the memories there. This is especially true in cases where the funeral was held in the church. Others have a struggle with the bombardment of "cheer up" statements they encounter. Too often, church members, including pastors, are convinced that quoting a scripture somehow heals your pain. They mean well and would not hurt you for the world, but they simply do not realize that telling you your loved one is in heaven does not bring them back to your side and that is all that would really help right now.

Too often the grief journey is made much more difficult and complicated by our not knowing how to respond to well-meaning people who want to help but have no idea what to say or who have a set platitude they say over and over. You cannot avoid all of them all of the time, so your grief experience will be a process of knowing how to let it go in one ear and out the other. If they are good enough friends, you can tell them that you do not need advice or reasons; all you really need is a friend to listen even when you sound crazy. If they are not a close friend, smile while you refuse to listen. A deaf ear is a valuable tool.

There is no such thing as "getting over" your grief. A chunk has been bitten out of your heart and it will not grow back. Hopefully you will turn the corner in the way you cope and learn to live again with a new reality. A reality with your loved one no longer being present in your life, but a new reality with the person being very present in your heart and in your memories. That is the journey of grief.

*I have a thought or feeling. I decide the thought or feeling is wrong.*
*Then I decide I should not have such thoughts or feelings.*
*I must be crazy, or I would not have them.*
*Therefore, I am crazy.*
*The result is that I feel bad because I feel bad.*

## Chapter 4

# The Right to Grieve

If you boiled down everything those of us who write about grief to one word, that word would be permission. We need permission to grieve. The name of this book says it all. We do not want people taking our grief away from us. We want someone to walk with us through the long nights and endless days of our grief without trying to fix it or take it away.

After the young mother said "Don't take my grief away from me," an experience and epiphany that changed my life, I started what must have been some of the first grief recovery groups ever. I had no idea what groups were or how they should function. I just gathered some grieving people together and listened to them as they searched for meaning and some relief from the pain of their losses. The one overriding issue was the struggle they were having with permission to grieve.

They felt tremendous pressure to either be over it, or act like they were. They felt pressure from every side. If they showed signs of grieving they thought folks looked on them as weak or, if at church, not having very much faith. They seemed to think everyone was watching them and judging every action. One lady said she needed a new car but would not buy one because she was sure people would be saying, "Her husband isn't even cold and there she is spending all of his money."

While some of the pressure we feel comes from our imaginations, a lot of it is very real. It can be subtle, hidden, and expressed in hints or very evident attitudes that tell us we should be able to put it behind us and move on long before we are ready to do so.

You may not hear the words "wallowing in your grief" said out loud but you will certainly sense them being thought. People may never actually say you have grieved long enough and it is time to get on with your life, but you will feel them counting the months and setting the parameters for how long you should hurt. They may never realize they are trivializing your grief when they say the classic, "God will not put more on you than you can bear," but you will feel it just the same. People who have not been through a grief experience themselves have no idea how deeply it hurts or how long it lasts. Many of them feel compelled to tell you how you should grieve even if they have never been there.

Some folks who have experienced grief may think they are the experts on the subject and will seek to guide you while insisting that you respond in the same way they did. There are no experts on grief. Grief is as unique as a finger print and everyone goes through it in their own unique way and on their unique schedule. So no one can be an expert in anyone else's grief. You will not grieve like anyone else and should not be pressured to try. Do it your way.

Perhaps the hardest permission of all is the permission we give ourselves. It is easy to fall victim to the "feel bad because we feel bad" syndrome. That happens when we have a bad day and tell ourselves we should not feel the way we do. The next step is to tell ourselves there is something wrong with us or we would not feel the way we do. Followed by therefore there is something wrong with us and it all snowballs into panic and self pressure to feel differently than we do.

Maybe the most helpful thing I could do for you is to say: If you had a broken leg and the doctor put you in a cast for eight weeks you would wear the cast without beating yourself up that you should be well sooner or not need the cast. If, at the end of eight weeks, the doctor said the leg was not healed and needed eight more weeks, you would be sad but you would not think you were just being weak and a sissy. The fact that the leg is broken and is slow to heal does not prove anything about you.

But when our hearts are broken, we somehow think we should heal almost over night. If we don't, we begin to judge ourselves as weak or of little faith or just being silly. If you are not careful, you will begin to tell yourself that you should be doing better than you are and begin to worry about your mental and emotional stability.

May I simply say, your heart has been crushed? It will take a long time before you are able to cope no matter how strong you are nor how much faith you have. During that long time you will think you are half crazy at times, you will not think straight at other times. You will cry at the weirdest times without warning. You will feel pain you could never imagine. There will be times when you feel too good and that, too, will be scary. There is a "feel bad because you *don't* feel bad" syndrome as well and it is as scary as the other.

Nothing will make the healing move faster nor take the pain away. This journey must be walked through; there is no way around it. You can deaden the pain with pills or drink but when they wear off the pain will still be there demanding your attention. If you fight yourself and your feelings, it makes things take longer and uses up too much energy trying to control how you feel.

It is very hard to do, but the secret is to give yourself permission to grieve for as long as necessary until you can live again. The best advice I can give is feel what you feel. You cannot change the feelings and trying to do so saps your energy, so allow yourself to feel what you feel until the feelings change. They will change. I promise.

*The path is not smooth or even well marked.*

# Chapter 5

# Grief On the Run

The struggle with grief would be much shorter and far less painful if we could go off in a cave somewhere with one or two people who understand us and nurture us back to health. Or if there was some rehab center we could check in to for a few months so we could stay away from all other cares and demands so we could concentrate solely on dealing with all of the emotions and transitions we must face in this journey. There is no cave nor is there a rehab center. We must deal with our grieving on the run while life goes on. We grieve in snitches and snatches while dealing with our lives.

Life does not stop and wait for us to get strong enough to deal with it. The normal challenges of every day life keep happening. The demands of our jobs may let up for a very brief moment, but very soon we are expected to perform as usual. If we do not do so we can sense the pressure building and the criticisms flowing beyond our hearing.

Our social structure is not designed for grief. Businesses tend to give employees a few days off during and right after the funeral and expect them to be running on all cylinders as soon as they return. Most of us could go back to work a couple of days after the funeral easier than we can a week or so later. It takes time for grief to become real. We need time off when reality begins to hit much more than we do right after the funeral. I wish companies would allow employees to return as soon as they feel they can and then offer a week or so of bereavement leave about three weeks later. That is more likely to be when the real pain starts and we are back at work by then and expected to be up to speed.

Grief on the run may be the reason grief comes in waves that seem to overwhelm us. The waves hit when they choose and usually at very inappropriate times. I cannot recount the times someone told me of having to leave a half-full grocery cart in the aisle and just go home because a wave hit without reason or warning and they could not control the tears. Sometimes we can understand what caused the wave. Most of the time we have no clue. My theory is that grief builds up while we are on the run and explodes when the pressure gets too great. Too many of our tears are spilled in public when we are embarrassed and try our best to stifle the flow. Tears are memories in motion and very important to our grieving process. They need to flow unabated but it is hard to find the time and place while we are forced to grieve in the midst of life.

It might be helpful for you to set up some kind of structured time when you will find a quiet place to think and feel. If you have a mate who could join you at this set time with the understanding that you are there for a quiet time of reflection and tears that could even be better, but having company in your quiet time should be your choice. We will talk about the family dynamics later in the book, but it also is important to set aside a time for the family to grieve together. Scheduling can be challenging, of course. Our lives are so full and busy that it might not be possible. In our family I tried to have a personal word with each of my daughters. Most of the time these were passing moments, but at least we tried to keep in touch with where each person was on their own journey and how they were feeling. On the one hand that feels inadequate, but the inadequacies are the result of our world of grieving on the run.

Most of us will not get to complete our transitions through one grieving experience before we have to face another. Other deaths happen; we lose a job; our health breaks, or the death made the family face long term care choices. Some folks refer to that as complicated grief. I have a problem with that description because all grief is complicated, but it does show how difficult it is to maintain two losses at the same time. Grief cannot be grouped together and dealt with as a package of losses. We need to deal with each one and the grief following each will differ because the relationship differed. Finding ways to separate them is necessary, but not easy.

Four months after my wife died, I lost enough of my eyesight to require me to quit driving. That decision forced some major changes in my lifestyle, none of which were desired or welcomed. Living alone without a car changes everything—period. That is a grieving experience. Suddenly I had two things to mourn. They are certainly different and my responses were different. I mourned the loss of my wife. I cussed and raved over the loss of my driving. Both were forms of grieving. When a wave hit I would stop and try to figure out which one I was crying over. Somehow I felt the need to understand which one was causing the tears at that time. I don't know why I did that. It may be that I was unconsciously keeping score to ensure that I gave the right amount of tears to the loss of my wife.

There is nothing we can do about the fact that we must grieve on the run or that we probably don't get to deal with our losses one at a time. It may help you to recognize this as reality and know that these facts will impact your journey. The path is not smooth or even well marked. Somehow individuals have been walking this way since there were people. We stumble a lot. We don't always do it right, if there is a right. But I really believe it is possible to learn to cope and live again even though it would be so much easier in a cave.

*How you react and how you
express how you feel
needs to fit who you are
and how you relate.*

## Chapter 6

# There Is No Right Way

I have studied grief for well over thirty years. I have written books and presented innumerable speeches and seminars on the subject. I have listened to thousands of people as they told the story of their loss and their grief, and yet, there I was wondering if I was doing it right. Was I crying as much as I should? Did I feel as much pain as my loss should cause? Was it normal to feel comfortable living alone? Should I have been ready to date or seek a new relationship? Should I have felt guilty if I did? How long am I supposed to wait?

There is no pattern for grief to follow. We can write about some very general things you might experience, but no one fits them in the same way or on the same schedule. We are individuals with unique ways of seeing and reacting to life itself which means we will react to both the pleasures and the pains of life in our own way. Matter of fact, we will respond to pain with about the same emotions and intensity that we do to pleasure.

Some folks get rather giddy about good news and good events. They have the ability to be free with their emotions and to show them with great intensity. Others react to the same events with almost detached emotions. Both enjoyed the event to the same degree they just expressed their joy in totally different ways. Sometimes the exuberant ones wonder if the silent ones enjoyed it at all, while the silent ones may wonder how the others could be so silly. We respond out of how we are built and how our environment has taught us to react to both pain and pleasure.

The result is that everyone goes through grief in their own individualized way, but, since there is no set pattern, most people are left wondering if they are doing it right. I don't know that I have ever talked to a single person that did not question the way they were grieving. I must say I was rather surprised when I began to question, just like everyone else. I thought all of my experiences with others would have prepared me to accept my grieving no matter what course it took.

If it feels right to you then it probably is right. That is a dangerous statement because it opens up the opportunity for those who try to avoid grieving all together to keep living in denial and tell the world they have done their grieving. This does not mean it is alright to avoid. It simply says if you are facing the loss and dealing with the feelings then how you react and how you express how you feel needs to fit who you are and how you relate. If it does so, then relax and let it take its normal course.

*Survival is the basic need of our lives.
If someone yells that the building is
on fire, our first instinct
is to get ourselves
to safety.*

# Chapter 7

# First You Must Survive

The first days of grief feel very selfish. We think of ourselves and our loss far more than we think of the person who died or even the pain the rest of the family might be facing. The wife of a friend of mine died very suddenly following successful surgery. I was out of town and did not know until three weeks after her death. We met for lunch as soon as possible and the first words he said to me were:

> There must be something wrong with me. All I think about is me. I wake up in the night wondering who I could marry, and I don't want to get married. It is all about me. Why? When will I think about my wife or my children? Why am I being so selfish and self centered?

I tried to help him understand that he was not being selfish; he was just trying to survive. Survival is far different from selfishness. Survival is the basic need of our lives. If someone yells that the building is on fire, our first instinct is to get ourselves to safety. When a death happens the first thing we think about is what will happen to me? Who will take care of me? How will I live? Can I stand the pain?

I talked about this at a conference and a young woman said, "I am glad you explained that. When my grandmother died my grandfather said, 'Who will cook for me now?' and I thought he was a selfish old bird, but he was just expressing his loss in terms of impacts he could understand."

The first part of the grieving process is our understanding of what we have lost and we need others to understand as well. We want to tell our story and for friends and family to grasp the depth of our loss and our pain. We tell the story of how the loved one died, where we were, and how it hit us. It becomes vitally important that others know, but in reality we are establishing this loss and the impact on our lives to ourselves. As we talk it become real to us, and we can begin to deal with the total impact only when it has become real. It is healing then to tell and understand, "This is what I have lost."

Very soon the day will come when you will want the world to know about the person you have lost, but right now you need to deal with the personal side of the loss. You need to think through and understand the depth and breadth of the loss to your life and tell your story at every opportunity. It is almost as if things will be better when everyone possible has a grasp what has happened to you. Like my great-grandson coming to the office after a cast was put on his broken arm. He very carefully went to each person to show them his cast and tell them how it happened and how much it hurt. Somehow he felt better when each person stopped to look and listen. That is the first step in your survival and your survival must be first on your list.

*A cut finger—*
*is numb before it bleeds,*
*it bleeds before it hurts,*
*it hurts until it begins to heal,*
*it forms a scab and itches until*
*finally, the scab is gone and a*
*small scar is left where once there*
*was a wound.*
*Grief is the deepest wound you have*
*ever had. Like a cut finger, it goes*
*through the process of healing*
*and leaves a scar.*

# Chapter 8

# Understanding Grief

There were very few books on grief in 1979 when the first edition of this book was written. I read every book I could find, and sought out other literature in a vain search for information about the grieving process. No one was writing much on the subject at that time. Elizabeth Kubler-Ross did some research on death and developed descriptions of stages she observed people passing through as they approach death. Like all the other authors at the time, I adapted her stages of death to the stages of grief and had a nice little outline of what a person goes through when we face a loss. We all used these stages in writing and speaking for several years until we finally had to admit that there is no such thing as stages of grief. There is no set pattern which needs to be or must be followed as we progress in the grief experience.

I was never very comfortable with the idea of stages. They sounded too clear cut and defined. I was afraid folks would spend too much time and energy trying to determine which stage they were in. I always thought we flip flopped through the stages. We could be in stage two this morning and back to stage one by afternoon. I even thought we could be in two stages at the same time. I looked for a different way to describe the process and have used several over the years. I have written that grief is like peeling an onion, it comes off one layer at a time and you cry a lot. That may be my favorite but it, too, presents the process as defined periods of time and thought. Maybe it would be a better idea to just list some of the feelings or responses that seem to be prevalent in most people at some time in their grief. This does not mean that you must experience all of them and certainly does not mean you must experience them in any order. From listening to the stories of so many people over the years it seems to me that we usually have periods of feeling and reacting in some of the ways listed here.

## A Time of Shock and Denial

The mind will protect itself from going crazy even if it has to refuse to see what is right in front of it, or even if it has to shut down. When a death comes we tend to go into a time of shock and denial. Not denial that says it did not happen but a state of denial that refuses to see the reality and finality of the death. The mind tends to let us discover the reality slowly over a period of time. We know it happened but it just isn't real. I remember a mother saying, "I am sitting here planning my son's funeral, but I expect that door to open at any moment and for him to walk in as if nothing had happened."

Usually we go through the funeral planning and even the funeral itself in some kind of zombie state. We hurt. We cry. We recognize the finality of the event and yet it seems more like a nightmare we will awaken from soon and things will be back as they were.

There is no way to judge how long the denial lasts. It varies with each individual. I have known people who seemed to deal with their loss in reality and move on only to wake up months later with the actual reality suddenly dawning upon them.

Children have a wonderful ability to put things on hold and face reality on their own schedule. A mother called me deeply concerned about her thirteen-year-old daughter. The father had died when the girl was nine. The family did a good job of walking through their grief and the girl had gone to a grief recovery program. On the way to the orthodontist to get her braces off the girl began to cry. When asked what was the matter she said, "No one told me they never come back." The mother wondered if they had failed in some way to help her with her grief. I think there were two issues at work. First the reality and finality were becoming real in a new way at a time when she wanted her father to be there. The second issue was the fact that children do the grief of their age group at the time and tend to pick it up later to do the grief of that age until they complete the process. A nine-year-old girl did nine-year-old grieving. At thirteen she was able to pick it up and do some more, which seems very healthy.

Sometimes the delay in facing reality has other causes. When my father died, I did not feel anything. It was not so much a time of denial as an absence of feelings. I did not understand and felt a great deal of guilt wondering if I had stopped loving him. Eight months later I woke up one night reliving his death and began a much delayed grief. I now understand what happened. My father died after a long-term illness that demanded a great deal of care from me. When he died I was too exhausted to grieve. I had no emotions left to grieve with. I had to recover some before I could deal with the reality of his death. I have since learned that my experience was far from unique. Many individuals find their grief delayed after a loved one dies from a long-term and demanding illness. They are not relieved at the death so much as they are just exhausted.

Adults face reality in various ways and various schedules. There is no time limit. Grief is not a contest to see who can get through it fastest. It helps to know that these feelings are normal and will pass in their own time.

## When the Whirl Stops

The period of denial can best be described as a whirl. Questions are whirling in our minds but they pass before we can even ask. Feelings whiz by unannounced and unfelt. Reality is in there somewhere but it goes on by. For weeks after my brother died the thought that I would never see him again flew by, but it was gone before I could begin to really believe it.

But one day the whirl stops and the reality and questions no longer whiz by. They land and refuse to go away. In some cases the chest hurts and breathing becomes difficult. Many folks report that they are amazed at how much physical pain can accompany grief. They actually hurt when the whirl stops.

Others find the whirl stops more gradually and they do not experience the physical pain. Both are normal and neither cared for their loved one more or less than the other. Different people react to things in different ways.

Whether the whirl stops with suddenness and intensity or gradually over time, the results are the same. You begin to face the actuality of the loss. This is the hardest part of the grieving experience. The loneliness seems overwhelming. The fears can haunt day and night. The guilt, the anxiety, the anger, and more feelings than I can list, crash in on minds and emotions.

There is no way to determine how long this time of intensity will last. It depends on the relationship you had with the loved one, the type of death and, to a greater extent, how much support you have or allow. The feelings need to be talked through almost one by one until you have worn the hard edges off and can handle them with less pain.

## Let Me Tell You of My Love

At some point you add a new emphasis to your story. At first you want the world to know about your loss and how it impacts your life. It is so important for each person to do so and for someone to hear and understand, that you really can't move on in your journey until you get the story told. Gradually you begin to feel the need to tell the world about the person you have lost. You want to be sure the person is honored appropriately and not forgotten.

On one of my trips to New York after the September 11, 2001 attacks, it seemed that people just lined up to tell their stories. There were too many stories there and not enough ears. One young woman handed me a laminated picture of her husband who was a fireman. She talked fast while I tried to read the information at the bottom of the picture. When she finished, I handed the picture back to her and she said, "Oh no keep it! I have hundreds of them." Evidently she had hundreds of pictures to show to anyone she could grab. She wanted the world to know about her husband and his life. She wanted his life remembered. She is not alone. Most of us at some point in the grieving process begin to feel the need to tell the story and ensure the honor of our loved one.

There is another reason for us to do this. The fact is we do not know the value of our loved ones either. You do not know the value of what you have until it is gone. We do not know what our loved one meant to us until they are gone. It is almost like we have to inventory the loss before we can grieve it. I fully intended to die first just so I would not have to go through this part of the process. Every day you think of something else you wanted to ask them. Every day you think of something else they did for you that will no longer be done. Every day you think of something else you wanted to do with them or for them and realize that will never happen. This is when the grief becomes real on the practical everyday life level. During this time grief becomes a process of discovering the value and telling others what you have discovered.

## How High is Your Bottom?

Alcoholics talk about the need to hit bottom before you can start back up and they talk about who has a high bottom and who has a low bottom. What they are referring to is the fact that some people recognize their problem before the disease almost takes over their lives while others never acknowledge it until they have lost almost everything they hold dear. That is far more dramatic than what we experience in our grieving, but the analogy is the same. In grief we gradually hit bottom and start building our lives back.

This takes much longer and is far more dramatic for some while others seem to begin the process of coping quite early and it seems just a natural step for them to take. Others take much longer and plum the depths of depression and despair in the process. All losses are not equal. Relationships vary greatly and we all respond to losses out of who we are.

Most people in grief are low bottoms. It seems that the pain gets worse instead of better. Milestones and anniversaries that we thought would make a difference pass and we see no progress. Time is supposed to heal but, if it does, it sure goes about it in a strange and inefficient way. Sometimes it comes to a head in a horrible wave of grief that seems worse than any before and we just don't think we can go on. From the depths we begin to realize that we must struggle back. We cannot stay there. Some even get angry and the anger becomes the driving force toward adjusting and coping. We will talk about anger more fully in later chapters. Whatever the force there comes a time when we begin to react to our grief and struggle toward health. No one can tell you when that will happen or what will cause it to happen, just know that the day will come when you begin the long climb out of the depths.

# Turning The Corner

It may seem impossible right now but a day will come when you will turn the corner in the way you cope with your loss. That does not mean you will be well and will not grieve this loss anymore. You will miss and long for their presence for as long as you live. Anniversaries, holidays, and sometimes just any day, will bring it back for a time but it will not be as devastating as it is now and you will be able to cope. Every time a friend or family member dies the grief will come back and you will work through the feelings again.

Turning the corner can be quite a dramatic event, or at least enough of an event for you to recognize something is happening. Usually we know when it happens. It can be a simple event like a friend of mine whose husband had died. She said on a Sunday morning she was walking to the parking lot after church and it suddenly hit her that she had to decide right then whether to live or die. She decided to live. It can be clothing or a chair the loved one sat in. Sometimes it is a child's room no one can touch. Usually there is something you cannot part with until that day and now you can.

I was surprised to discover the things I could not deal with for quite some time after my wife's death. I gave most of her clothes to her sister, and that felt very good to do so. The rest went to a charity she had followed and supported. That also felt good. One day I was cleaning out my own closet, and I decided this would be a good time to clear out her undergarments and pajamas. There is no place to donate these kinds of things, so they were to be discarded like my old shorts and socks. I opened the drawer without giving it a thought. I could not touch a single thing and closed the drawer. It took a while before I could open it and clean it out. That was my "turning the corner" day.

*It is a simple thing but the candle burning seems to remind us that he is alive in our hearts and with us in our joy.*

## Chapter 9

# A Series of Firsts

Grief forces us to face a series of firsts. The first time we do almost anything after the death can cause us to catch our breath and reflect on the loss or fall apart in a wave of grieving. It can be as simple as the first time we laugh and catch ourselves wondering if we should be doing so and if that is failing to show proper love and respect for the loved one, or as complicated as beginning to date after a spouse dies or having another baby after the loss of a child.

Some of the firsts are logical and evident, like the first time we face any anniversary: anniversary of a birth, anniversary of marriage, and of course the anniversary of the death. I have noticed a pattern to the way we seem to face these firsts. The anticipation of the event may be even worse than the event itself. We tend to start dreading the event about a month beforehand. We may not notice or make a connection to the upcoming event but something starts happening inside of us. We can become irritable for no known reason, begin having more difficulty sleeping, and feeling some unnamed sense of foreboding for a couple of weeks before we begin to realize an anniversary is coming and that must be the cause of the strange feelings and reactions we are experiencing. The anticipation can grow as we dread facing the day. Quite often the day comes and seems not to be as difficult as the dreading of it was.

For those facing the holidays for the first time after a death there is little gratitude on Thanksgiving and no jolly in Christmas. These are family oriented events that can become stark reminders that a loved one was here last year and not here this one. Most families have long standing traditions for celebrating these days and tend to want to continue the traditions without change while the grieving part of the family feel the loss is being forgotten and the love one's absence ignored.

At least in the immediate family, the traditions may need to change. If, for example, the family always hung stockings from the fireplace, the dilemma becomes should we hang all but the one belonging to the deceased and let the empty spot haunt us, or hang them all and act like nothing has happened? I think it wise to at least consider a dramatic change for the first Thanksgiving, Christmas, Hanukkah, or whatever holidays you celebrate. At least it should be something the family talks about beforehand.

There are a couple of issues that should be understood no matter what the family decides to do for the first holidays. First, a bereaved person should not be expected to perform the same duties as before. For example, if a woman always cooked the turkey for the holiday meal, at the holiday following the death of her husband, she should only do so if she feels like it and insists. There should be the possibility of other arrangements and she should never be made to feel any guilt.

The second thing that we need to watch is to be sure the loved one is fully acknowledged. When we are in grief we are super sensitive to the loved one's presence being recognized and honored. Our family suffered the death of a grandson who was born on Christmas Eve and died on Christmas day. Every Christmas since that day we have stopped to light a candle in his honor before we open any presents or proceed with the activities of the day. That is a simple thing but the candle burning seems to remind us that he is alive in our hearts and with us in our joy.

One of the most jarring "firsts" can be the first time you realize you have not thought of your loved one for the past several moments. At first we can think of nothing else. It is like the person is camped right before our eyes and on our minds 24/7. We become almost divided between thinking of our loved one while we sort of think about anything else we are forced to give some of our attention. It is easy to assume that their being constantly on our mind is our new normal and that is how it will always be. Then one day we notice that we have not thought of our loved one for a period of time. That can be scary. Are we forgetting them? Is it normal to have this kind of lapse in our concentration?

I have watched grieving people almost drum up their pain for fear that they were forgetting the person or not grieving as much as they should for the person. Sometimes we feel closer to the person when we are hurting and become afraid not to hurt.

The grief journey is a process of moving from the person being in front of our minds, to being a presence we feel in our hearts. That happens when we can become comfortable with not thinking about them all of the time and allow the process to move from their being in front of our face to being alive in our memories and quietly walking beside us through our days.

*Grief is as unique
as a fingerprint.*

# Chapter 10

# There Are No Comparisons

Just as there is no way to describe or define grief in a way that fits everyone, there is no way to compare the grief that results from each type of loss. In a very broad sense grief is grief and everyone experiences many of the same feelings and pains, but there is no way to compare the loss of a child with the loss of a long term spouse. Not that one is more important or even more painful, but each type of loss requires different adjustments and transitions. Each one has certain elements that are more prevalent and prominent than what is found in other losses. The elements are in each loss but can be more pronounced in some than in others. I cannot begin to understand the elements in each type of loss, much less define them. I can give enough examples to at least show there are differences.

## Pregnancy Loss

A person suffering a pregnancy loss through stillbirth or a miscarriage might feel more lonely and isolated. The mother is the only one who knew the child. She bonded at the moment of conception and has imagined a personality and a future long before the due date of the birth.

The husband has a bond as well and perhaps has felt the child move in the womb, but even he does not know the child as well as the mother. She must try to explain the value of the life to a world that has no idea about the child and, far too often, these losses are looked upon as minor grief and the mother is expected to get over the death in mere days and go on with life. In too many cases there is not even a memorial service or a place of burial. Even in the case of stillborn children the parents may not have had a chance to hold or even be with the child. They are left with empty arms and over active imaginations.

I visited a cemetery in Canada where a remarkable funeral director had purchased a large granite marker which simply said, "For all the unnamed babies." He offered to place the names of the families of stillbirths and miscarriages who were never memorialized. The first request for a name to be on the marker came from a seventy-five-year-old man who told of a son born long ago and never named. He was thrilled to have a place to honor the son, but was very sad that his wife did not live to see it. The last time I heard from the funeral director they had filled both sides of the marker and had ordered two more along with a bench to form a small park where people could gather. There are always balloons and toys left there, the result of someone trying to grieve through the loneliness and isolation.

## The Death of a Child

How could any grief compare with that following the death of a child? I lost a wife after fifty-seven years of a great marriage but still stand in awe of those who have had to face this gut wrenching loss. The questioning of why, the sense of it not being fair, the watching all of the friends still have their children and the physical pain of that death is far beyond my imagination. The intense grieving may gradually lessen but the loss lingers for life and is renewed at every possible natural event that should have happened. The class graduates from school and the child would have been there. Classmates get married and have children and the parents are reminded again and again that that will never happen for their child.

There is an old Yiddish proverb that says, "When a woman loses a husband she is called a widow. When a man loses a wife he is called a widower. When a child loses a parent they are called an orphan. But, there is no word for when a parent loses a child. That pain is far too great for words."

## When a Spouse Dies

The loss of a spouse throws the entire life into transition. Society has become so complicated that the first months after the death are full of sending death certificates to what seems like the entire world, taking care of bank accounts, insurance and taxes until there is seldom time to breathe, much less mourn. We have already covered the fact that we grieve on the run and all these tasks are done in the middle of the running. A wife must suddenly assume business matters she may not be equipped to handle. A husband may find himself totally baffled by the washing machine he never used before. Everything changes and it does so when our minds are not working and our hearts are bleeding.

Our society is geared for couples and the loss of the other half of the relationship can be magnified and intensified. Learning how to eat alone, go to parties or movies as a single, or just sitting in the house without conversation can all be daunting tasks. One lady called our office to buy some books and said, "You watch others go through losing a mate and think they should be able to handle it. Until it happens to you. I had no idea how hard it would be. No idea!"

## When a Parent Dies

Because the relationships and situations are so varied, it is impossible to describe or define the grief from the death of a parent. The feelings and responses run the gamut from losing the very rudder that has guided our lives, to the end of a lifelong struggle for love and peace.

The responses are also governed by the physical situations we face with aging parents as opposed to the loss of a parent at a too young age. Long-term care can leave us exhausted and convinced we have already grieved the loss long before the death happens, only to discover that grief cannot be grieved in advance. The loss of a young and vibrant parent seems so unfair and leaves us devastated.

I cannot list the number of times I have heard, or even said it myself, when trying to explain some complicated life, "Well, her mother died when she was very young, or his dad died when he was seven." Saying the words seems to explain so much about the person. We instinctively know that losing a parent imprints our lives.

When there has been a lifelong struggle for acceptance and love, the death leaves us with far too many unfinished agendas that become much harder to work through.

All of these issues impact the way we grieve and often the length of the journey, but they do not remove the grief. When a parent dies a hole is left in our lives. Something very important is no longer there. The final human security is gone, and we feel hollow and alone. There is no longer the safety net we always knew would be there no matter how far we fell.

We not only lose the parent, most likely we also lose the home. When a house becomes a home it takes on meaning and memories that we cannot give up with a shrug. It is home and the things there are there because they had an impact on our lives and we felt a sense of security there among them that cannot be duplicated anywhere else. Mom, Dad, the home, the things, the memories all are losses we must grieve when a parent dies.

## Suicide

Suicide leaves a family shattered. Suddenly they are trying to make sense of a thousand piece jig saw puzzle with missing pieces and no picture on the box to guide them. It is almost like they must put the puzzle together before anyone can stop and grieve. Why did this happen? What caused it? Why did we not see it coming? Who is to blame? These major questions dominate and there is rarely an answer for any of them.

I walked with a couple whose thirteen-year-old son died of suicide. The father happened to be a physician and the mother a nurse. They spent the first year researching every medicine the boy had taken, every possible thing that could have had a negative impact on their son. Every word they had said to him in the months before he died. Finally, when they had exhausted every avenue they had to face the overwhelming fact that they would never have the answers they craved and allowed themselves to begin facing their grief. As I wrote earlier, having answers does not make the pain go away. The bottom line is the loved one is not here and we must learn to live with them not being here.

## Violent Death

The murder of a loved one begins a never ending ordeal of waiting before you can stop and grieve. There seems to be no way for the family to give into the natural process of grieving until the person who committed the crime is caught and sometimes that takes years or never happens at all. If the person is caught the grief seems to be on hold until after the trial, which is a grief experience within itself. The anger, the lack of justice, the horror the loved one felt, the shame one might feel for no good reason all seem to dominate and control the process of dealing with the feelings of grief. Few families ever really complete the journey.

## Grieving What You Never Had

I visited with three sisters in the waiting room of a hospital as their mother was dying. I had known them for a long time but had no idea how much anger they felt toward their mother. They informed me that they had no intention of having a funeral for her when she died. They felt like she had never loved them and they saw no reason to act like they were grieving over her loss. I asked them to at least have a family story telling time and offered to have it at my home. They agreed. When they arrived I said, "Not every mother is loving, nor is every father warm and caring. Everyone who dies is not necessarily a good person or a good parent. Sometimes we must grieve that which we never had and wished we had." That, too, is grief, difficult to express of course, and not pretty to listen to, but necessary nonetheless.

They shared their anger and frustration for several minutes and one could feel the anger gradually bleed off as they talked. Harsh words were said, but what else could they do with harsh words? If they were not spoken they would have festered inside of them and become depression or something worse. Not all people are loved or loving. Grieving is expressing whatever is there, and sometimes it is a time of finishing some long held unfinished agendas. That kind of grieving is healing also.

Those are just examples. What about your grief? Since grief is as unique as a fingerprint, yours does not fit any of the above, and there is no way to compare yours with others. Each death impacts different people in a way that fits only them and the relationship that existed between the two people involved. Yours, then, fits only you. Perhaps it would be helpful for you to write out a description of your unique grief. Writing helps order the mind and gives a perspective of the experience as a whole. Somehow seeing it from that angle can help you in your journey. Good luck.

*Knowing what is normal is one of the most important helps we can find.*

# Chapter 11

# Why Am I So Tired?

In my part of the world we have two words for being tired. There is tired and then there is "tard". "Tard" is tired to the second power. You will understand that word as you make the long journey through your grief. As we have already discussed, grief comes in waves that seem to overwhelm us. When a wave hits, the body secretes a hormone called cortisol which the body uses as protection from stress. Grief is not the only trigger for this hormone but it does fire during an intense wave of its presence.

The cortisol seems to fill us and then gradually bleed off as we talk or even as we cry only to return at the next wave and fill us up again. The body has several reactions to the filling.

The hormone makes it difficult to concentrate. You may think you have had a sudden attack of attention deficit disorder. The mind just won't stay hitched for very long. I do not write large books about grief simply for that reason. A grieving person will find it hard to even open a large book with a lot of words to read. It overwhelms them. A church group showed me their grief recovery program and I shuddered. It was a very large notebook with videos, workbooks and papers to be read. Probably good material but during their time of greatest need most grieving people just can't concentrate long enough to even open the notebook.

You have to get your information in short bursts. Anything long and complicated is beyond your ability to fathom. This means you have not lost your mind or your ability to read and comprehend. You have not suddenly become mentally deficient. It just means the cortisol that goes along with stress and grief makes it hard for anyone to concentrate or even think through thoughts long enough to reach conclusions.

It is not unusual for people to experience "brown out" during grief. The mind just doesn't work like it did and it is easy to decide you are going crazy. Some time after my brother died, my sister-in-law called late one night. She was laughing to hide her concern. She said she must be going crazy. She had been searching her home trying to find a certain lamp. She had two brass lamps and one was missing. She had looked for several days and could not imagine where the lamp could have gone. That night, just before she called me, she found the lamp. It was on the table beside her and she had been reading by it ever since it disappeared. She said she had actually turned that lamp off and gone to look for it. No wonder she was worried about her sanity or at least creeping dementia. I explained "brown out" and told her to wait. Her mind would work again.

The cortisol zaps your energy. Part of this comes from the fact that it dehydrates you which, in turn, makes you tire easier. It took me several weeks to recognize that the tiredness I was feeling was connected to the grief I was experiencing. I thought I was just suddenly old. I call it "tard" because there does not seem to be any way to get rested. A good night's sleep doesn't seem to do as much good as it once did. We seem to run out of gas earlier than usual and can't find the second gear we once could rely on to pull us through.

The important thing is to recognize both the symptoms and the cause. In grief it is important for you not to panic and decide there is something wrong. Knowing what is normal is one of the most important helps we can find. It is also important to know that all of this will pass. The waves will lessen in both the regularity and the intensity. The body will calm down and your mind and strength will return.

*I wonder—*
*Does God gossip?*
*Does He talk to other folks*
    *about me?*
*If not, why do they think they know*
    *His way for me?*
*If He does,*
    *I wish he would quit it.*

# Chapter 12

# Feel What You Feel

She came to my office to talk about a religious problem. She was convinced she no longer had any faith. She hated church, did not feel as if prayer did any good, was envious of people who seemed to have it all together, and seemed to be plagued with what she called "bad thoughts."

It was almost an hour before she slowed the conversation down enough for me to ask any questions. During this hour she outlined enough sins to ruin all of the saints in heaven. She was a terrible person in her own mind. She had thought of herself as being a very religious person and then everything just fell apart after her husband died.

After he died she felt pressure to carry on with bravery and faith. She enjoyed the people remarking about how strong she was. Going back to church alone was one of the hardest things she had ever done, but she did it. She was ready to tell anyone how her faith had conquered her grief and she had the victory. Even while she was speaking of victory her insides were screaming, "Not so."

She tried to dismiss those thoughts and cover her feelings.

Gradually she could not cover any more. The feelings inside were going to be heard no matter how much she fought to stifle them. She finally had to get honest with herself and face the reality of what she was feeling. Unfortunately, she could not accept the feelings as normal. She thought a person of faith never had bad feelings or bad thoughts.

She felt envious of other couples and told herself that jealousy was a sin.

She thought of herself and her problems and told herself she was selfish and that was wrong.

She tried to pray, could not do so, and told herself she had lost God.

She thought of sex and reacted with horror.

She was tempted to drink and was frightened by the temptation.

She hid all of these feelings. She tried to hide them from herself and then when she could do so no longer, she was determined to hide them from everyone else. She redoubled her efforts to appear well and happy.

Her particular religion seemed to put a great deal of pressure upon her. It seemed to say, "If you pray and read the Bible, you will have no problems." The more she prayed and read the Bible, the worse she felt. This led to even more feelings of guilt and unworthiness because it seemed to work for others and did not work for her.

Her faith talked a great deal about victory. The meetings she attended were all designed for folks to share the victories in their lives. She felt none.

All of these swallowed feelings left her depressed. Even the depression made her feel guilty. After all, a person of faith is not supposed to feel depressed. Her conclusion was that she had a religious problem. Her conclusion was that she was a bad person.

All of the hidden feelings had snowballed and she was convinced that she was a bad, weak, or crazy person and maybe all three. She was convinced that a normal person would not feel or think like she felt and thought. This lady's conclusion centered completely on her religion. Others can center on the idea of being mentally ill, or that of being weak or just an inadequate person.

I dealt with her by asking again and again how she was supposed to feel. When she would list for me all of the bad feelings and thoughts, I would just ask again, "How are you suppose to feel when your husband dies?" I explained to her that grief is a deep wound that needs time to heal and will not just go away, no matter how much religion she had. I said, "If you broke your leg, would you think it weak or nonreligious to be hurt until the leg healed? If not, why is it weak or nonreligious to hurt until grief heals?"

At first she protested, "But other people don't think like this."

I said, "At least they do not let you know they think like this."

She looked at me in utter disbelief. To her, I was attacking her religion.

Too often, religion only tells one side of the story. We share the victories with great gusto, but we rarely even talk about the defeats. One of the best things I ever did in church while serving as a minister was to have a testimony time when we shared our prayer defeats. Some of the very finest Christians stood to express fear and frustration for the first time in their lives. We all sat together and felt normal.

The "Victory Only" approach leaves us convinced everyone has much more faith than we do. It leaves us feeling as though we are the only ones who ever feel the way we feel or the only ones to ever think the thoughts we think. The truth is there are no super people. Most of us are about alike. Everyone has bad thoughts, angers, temptations, fears, and frustrations. If we could be honest with one another, we could feel normal. Since we cannot seem to be this honest, we feel everyone else is a super-religious person and we are spiritual peons.

This is also true outside of religion. Everyone else seems to have it all together while we feel the fears, angers, temptations, and frustrations of living. The longer I live the more convinced I am that underneath the façade we are all just human beings. We just don't let our humanness show.

When grief comes, feelings you never dreamed you had suddenly show up. Since we all play the game of never showing true feelings, we have no idea how others feel. Therefore, you do not really know how others feel. Since you do not know, it is easy to assume your feelings are odd or not proper. You can then decide that since you are thinking or feeling wrong there must be something wrong with you. The result is that you feel bad because you feel bad.

How are you supposed to feel in grief? What kind of feelings are normal? What is okay, and what is not okay? Maybe it is time for us to get honest.

## You are Going to be Selfish

Selfish is not the right word to use, but it is the word you will probably use to describe your situation. It will feel like selfishness. During grief you will think of yourself almost all of the time. Everything will be related to you. You may even resent anyone talking about someone else's problems. Inside you may cry out, "How dare you tell me of someone else's problem when I am hurting?"

If a person tells you how bad he or she feels because they do not know what to say, your reaction might be, "Here I am hurting, and all you can do is tell me how bad you feel—big deal."

These feelings are normal. This is how you should feel. There is no need to go off somewhere and kick yourself for being selfish.

This turning inward to your own needs is not selfishness—it is survival. When you are attacked your whole being goes into survival mode. This is a built-in defense mechanism. It is as natural as craving food when you are hungry. No one ever calls normal eating selfish. Eating is survival. Eating is necessary to staying alive.

Turning to your own needs in grief is also survival. It is also necessary to staying alive. When you have a headache, nothing else matters very much except the ache in your head; you cannot read, you cannot listen to others, and you cannot be very concerned about the hurts of others. Headaches dominate while they are there. Heartaches do the same. During the grief journey your whole system is trying to survive and recover. While this is going on you will be dominated by your own hurts and your own needs. Call this selfish if you want to; in reality it is simply surviving to live another day.

## You May Be Envious

How else could you feel if you have lost a mate and other couples seem to be so happy together? You must adjust to loneliness while they seem to flaunt their togetherness.

How else could you feel if your child has died and you see happy family groups enjoying life together? How could you be expected to be joyous at a wedding your child can never have? You are glad for the young couple and the family, but your insides will be aching.

The old statement, "I felt sorry because I had no shoes until I met a man who had no feet," sounds great but, frankly, in the middle of winter, I still want some shoes.

You can tell yourself a thousand times how wrong it is to be envious after a loss, but telling yourself won't make it go away. In time it will be less intense, but every happy event will bring it back to mind.

## You will Probably Think of Sex

This, of course, will depend on your own feelings and, perhaps, your age. There is no switch inside you that can be flipped to shut off the natural need for love, affection, and sex. Since God did not provide such a switch, He must understand that these feelings will be there, and you will think about them.

The need for love is as natural as the need for food. When this need is no longer being met, you cry out for it like crying for food when you are starving. Add to this the fact that every emotion you have has been turned upside down by the trauma of grief, and you can begin to see why these feelings and needs are intensified during this time. Again you are in survival mode. During survival all needs become big needs. This need is no exception.

So you may well be selfish, angry, envious, and tempted. Does this mean you are bad, or does it mean you are normal?

The answer is normal. You can face the thoughts and feelings and accept them as a normal part of grief. If you can accept them in this way, you can live with them and live through them. The feelings are bad enough without adding the tension and fear of non-acceptance.

If you do not accept these feelings and thoughts as normal you go to war with yourself. Energy needed for recovery is spent on self-hate. At the time you need the most support, you are not giving support to yourself. At the time you need every good word you can get you are receiving bad words from yourself. The result is that depression is deepened, fears are formed into guilt, and you become a bundle of self-loathing and judgement.

The best way to find a healing path in grief is found in the word "relax." If you take care of yourself and let the normal reaction s take their course, in time  you will find yourself looking back saying, "I survived."

*Until the feelings return it is a process of putting one foot in front of the other.*

# Chapter 13

# What Happened to My Want To?

A woman in deep grief told me the story of her husband's sudden death at a very young age. She was left with small children to raise and a business to run without being prepared to do either by herself. She asked me how she could hurt so badly on the one hand and be so numb on the other. She said:

> It sounds strange but sometimes the numbness is worse than the pain. I take care of the business but I am just functioning and running on adrenalin when I do so. I love my children but I do not have the same joy I have always felt while giving them care. I am dead inside.

As we talked I explained that the depression that usually accompanies grief does not just make us feel blue and sad, it can also leave us with no feelings, numb. It seems like it would be impossible to hurt and be numb at the same time, but we do. Our emotions are used up in the grieving and we have none left for normal living. We just don't feel the same way we did. We tend to feel emotionally flat and detached. It seems like we are off to the side watching ourselves go through the motions but not really being involved in the process.

I experienced a long period of this flatness on my grief journey. I still functioned and enjoyed what I do, but I did not feel the same lump in my throat I always felt when I prepared to make a speech or responded to someone in pain. I still cared and hoped I was still effective, but I longed for those feelings to return. I have always interpreted those feelings as inspiration and I missed them.

I cannot explain how empty that numbness makes us feel. We depend on our emotional responses for so much of what we do. Some more than others of course, but all of us need some internal response in order to feel like we are functioning properly.

Prayer is a good example of this need. Most of the people I have talked with have said they have some kind of feeling in their hearts when they pray that feels like a connection has been made between them and their God. If that is not there, prayer feels empty and that no connection has been established. It is like their prayers hit the ceiling and bounce back. I cannot count the number of people who have expressed how hard it was to pray while they were in grief.

If you are feeling numb, I have some good news to share. In time the feelings will return. It will be so gradual you may not notice it until one day you sort of wake up and realize you are feeling again. Even though I wrote those words and have expressed them to countless people, the return of my own feelings surprised me. As I was making a speech I noticed the lump in my throat had returned. I don't know when it happened, it was just there.

The feelings will return much faster if you don't fight yourself because they are not there. Constantly telling yourself that you should care more takes up too much energy at a time when energy is scarce.

Then comes the hard part. Until the feelings return, it is just a process of putting one foot in front of the other; doing your job, not because you feel inspired or joyous in doing so, but simply because it has to be done. That makes everything harder of course. Like the lady said, sometimes you hate the numbness more than the pain. It is not easy to function with no emotion. I longed for the day when I would feel the tug in my throat and the small hurt in my heart as I wrote and spoke. I knew it would come, but I am the kind of guy who prays, "Lord give me patience and give it to me right now!"

*Once I allowed myself to understand the process, I quit waking up and making a list.*

# Chapter 14

# The Urge to Merge

I have always believed that the first year of grieving was a poor time to make major decisions. Sometimes situations force us to do so, but I think it is better to wait until our emotions return and our minds begin to work again.

I have watched several of my friends, particularly male friends, marry very soon after the death of a mate. I have also observed that many of those marriages did not turn out very well. I must admit that I have seen some wonderfully happy unions from early marriages as well. I just don't think the odds are as good and recommend caution.

I have a friend who was engaged in three months, and married in six, after the death of his wife. They seem to have a fine marriage although he says they have had some hard adjustments in the process. Recently he asked me how long I thought it took to mourn the death of a spouse. I told him the rule of thumb that most who study grief talk about is two years. That does not mean a person hurts for two years, it just means it takes a long time for all of the emotions to return to normal and to work through all of the transitions involved. But, I said,

I think it must take longer if you marry quickly, and he agreed. It stands to reason that it would take longer simply because he is left with no safe place to grieve or no one to share it with. His new wife does not want to see him crying for his first wife, and telling his friends about his grieving is embarrassing since he is already once again happily married.

I have also had to walk with the children who feel resentment and rejection due to a father's early re-marriage. It seems to be a slap at their mother and cast doubt on the father's love for her. I am sure this is also true when a woman marries very soon after the death of a husband, but I have dealt with far more men than women in this kind of situation, so I feel better informed about men.

I do heartily recommend care in financial planning before marriage. Too often when someone rushes into marriage they do not take the time to really look at the future and are so much in love they think nothing could possibly go wrong. I have worked with too many children who found themselves cut off by the new wife and who ended up with very little or nothing when the father died before the second wife.

With all of that said, I had no idea why this happens so often until my wife died. Three weeks after her funeral I woke up one morning wondering who I could marry. I didn't want to get married but there I was forming a list of possibilities. Then I realized what was happening to me. When a mate dies, we seem to go into mating mode. It is a natural biological drive or instinct built in to us. Our instinct seems to kick in and drive us toward finding a new mate. This is an instinct or a biological urge.

It does not mean we are ready to marry or even that we want to.

I have watched this instinct cause some folks to turn on sexually, some to an extreme. Several of my women friends have gone through a time of promiscuity shortly after the death of their husbands. One very dedicated church attending woman had lived with a husband whose diabetes had killed his sexual drive and ability. She had not had sex in perhaps fifteen years and thought that drive was dead to her. She did not worry about this lack nor really even give it any thought, and then her husband died. A few weeks later she was in my office in a panic wondering if she had gone crazy and feeling like she had abandoned her God. She was having an affair with her husband's best friend and was almost insatiable. She could not believe me when I said that this was a natural reaction, at least it was natural for her, and that it would pass in time. She also could not believe that her God would ever understand. But who knows biological and natural urges better than the one who put us together?

The danger is that the sexual drive will overwhelm us and dominate us until all thoughts of grieving are put on the back burner and denied time and space. The first thing you know some otherwise sane men are buying convertibles and making fools of themselves. Somehow we need to realize these early feelings and urges are not really where we are or where we will be. Slow down and let nature restore sanity.

I am convinced that most of the early marriages happen because we interpret this urge as the need to marry and assume it is telling us we are ready. If we could understand what is really happening, take a deep breath and wait a while, the urge to merge will lessen or even go away. Once I allowed myself to understand the process I quit waking up making lists.

*Don't get behind
on your cussin'.*

## Chapter 15

# Keep Your Cussin' Current

Hang on to your hats, a minister is going to teach you how to cuss. Before you call the guardians of all that is good, let me explain. I use two words for expressing deep feelings. *Cursing,* in my world, is the use of foul language. The kind that demeans God or diminishes the value of other people. Racial and sexist remarks should be included in this gutter.

*Cussin'* is expressing feelings of anger in terms that fits the individual. Don't get behind in your cussin'.

It is obvious that grief creates tremendous amounts of negative feelings. It leaves you feeling forsaken, rejected, without answers, ignored, abandoned… the list could never be completed. All of these feelings come from the same emotion as anger, so I bundle them into that one word. There is anger in grief and there should be. Anger is the natural response to hurt. When someone or some situation hurts us, the most natural response is to get mad. We may not recognize what we feel as anger. Many people tell me they do not remember getting mad during their grief. When I say "Do you remember being hurt? Or rejected? Or unloved?" They usually say they remember those feelings but do not remember getting angry. We seem to avoid the word anger. Most of us were raised to believe it was wrong to get mad and we think of anger as lying in the floor holding one's breath and turning purple. That is a temper tantrum.

The anger of grief is more of an internal response. Maybe we should call it being upset. That term softens it and all of us can relate to being upset. I have even heard people say "I am not angry, I am just upset." Sounds and feels the same doesn't it? The anger is not only natural it is also healthy. The best thing to do with grief is grieve and the negative feelings drive the needed opportunities for mourning. These feelings are the basis of your sadness and tears. They cause the pain to well up and explode, which is a needed release. I cringe when I hear someone tell a grieving person they should not feel the way they feel. That is an effort to take away the person's grief instead of allowing the feelings to help them do the work of grief.

The anger becomes the driving force toward your learning to live again. We talked earlier about hitting bottom and beginning to fight back. People actually hit bottom and get mad enough to fight back.

Even though the anger is healthy it still needs to be dealt with. Swallowed anger becomes depression. We need to find outlets where we can blow off some steam without having someone try to "fix us." Sometimes having a place to scream helps. I served on the board of a grief recovery center for children. The facility had an "emotion commotion" room with padded walls and soundproofing where the kids could hit punching bags, swing padded bats and, in general, work off some of the built-up emotions of anger.

One lady told me she bought all the dishes she could find at garage sales. When her anger built up to a pitch, she would break the dishes into the dumpster in the alley.

Two friends of mine who had suffered the death of their sons put Easter eggs on golf tees and hit them all over the backyard. They said they planned to leave some un-boiled the following Easter and not know which ones so they could experience the splatter.

All of these feelings we are calling anger need to be expressed. Left alone the feelings tend to settle on someone or something. Unexpressed and unresolved feelings can build and we can find ourselves extremely angry at people or loved ones. Often there may be some basis for the anger to fixate there, but built up anger makes us far madder and more inconsolable than we should be.

I have watched the anger fixate on a mate and do terrible damage to a marriage. The anger is not expressed for fear of upsetting the mate until it builds into an explosion and words are said that are hard to ever take back.

There is no way to discover how many lawsuits are filed against doctors and hospitals after someone let their anger seethe until there was no way out except through the courthouse doors.

The same thing happens in anger aimed toward God. At first we dare not feel angry at the Eternal Being. Gradually we begin to let ourselves feel it, but dare not say it out loud so it is allowed to build and build until we are very angry at someone we cannot see and dare not talk about. We express our anger in questions like, "WHY?" or, if we dare, "Where was God when my loved one died?"

Strange as it may sound, all of these places to focus anger are healthy. They can create problems, of course, and can make us uncomfortable but at least we are finding a place for our anger to land and expressing it. We can work through the anger with our mates. We can figure out a way to settle lawsuits and God is big enough to handle our anger.

We are back to the word permission. The key to dealing with anger is permission to be angry. Most of us were not allowed to be angry when we were children and, too often, anger is looked on as a sign of character weakness and, in some religions, as a sin. The result is swallowed feelings and a lot of depressed people.

We need to keep our cussin' current. Anger needs to be expressed and expressed as early as possible and to the person who made us angry. Too often we tell everyone else and never confront the person involved. The only way to overcome an anger-causing situation is by confrontation that leads to understanding and healing.

Confrontation does not give you the right to attack the other person nor diminish their value. It just gives you the right to explain what happened and how that made you feel. Done early before the anger builds can result in a calm exchange. The other person may not respond, of course, but at least you have established your position and expressed your feelings.

Count to ten and then CUSS.

*"If onlys" block the
gifts of memories
that can sustain
you.*

## Chapter 16

# If Only

The most natural reaction in the world is to look for someone or something to blame when a hurt is present. You might fix the blame on the doctor, the hospital, the driver in the other car, or even on the person who died. It is human nature to need the blame established. As we discussed in the previous chapter, it is healthy and necessary to express your anger and your hurt in productive and healing ways so that it does not build up inside.

However, as many people do, you might have transferred the blame to yourself. "If only I had..." becomes the beginning phrase of most of your sentences.

If only I had been there.
If only I had forced him to go to the doctor.
If only I had been a better husband.
If only I had been a better wife.
If only I had been a better father.
If only I had been a better mother.
If only I had not let her drive that night.
If only I had listened and heard that there were dangerous feelings around.

If you are not careful, you may very quickly begin to fix guilt on yourself. If no guilt is there, you may manufacture some. Unfocused and unexpressed anger does not go away. Left alone it tends to internalize and we become angry with ourselves. I have been amazed at how often this happens. A lot of guilt we face in grief is really internalized anger that had no place else to go. In grief, people will build very elaborate scaffolds to prove it was their fault.

A young girl came to see me. Her story was one of the deeper tragedies I have ever dealt with. Her father had shot and killed her mother. In one horrible moment she had lost her mother by death and her father by his deed. You can imagine the feelings which ran through her mind and heart.

Where was my little friend going to place her feelings? She desperately fought to keep from feeling any stronger anger against her father than she already felt. She needed him now more than ever. He could not be with her, of course, but he was all she had. She was going to have a terrible time forgiving him or loving him without adding all of the anger and hurt to the relationship.

She shifted the blame to herself with an amazing fantasy. If she had gone to get her mother from work, her father would not have been there to meet her mother, and this would not have happened. If she had not overslept, she might have gone to get her mother. If she had been a better daughter, her mother would be alive. She had enough "if onlys" to last a lifetime. She had enough to make that lifetime miserable.

Are you at this point? Have you built up some "if onlys?" If so, you need to think through them very carefully. Most of the "if onlys" are not really true. Even the ones that are true are beyond your control. There is nothing that can be done to change the situation, the scenario, or the result. Just like my little friend, the hurt and anger inside needs a place to fix the blame. You have elected yourself to be that place.

It is much better if you can admit that you are angry, that you are hurt and that it is an expected and normal feeling. You should have these feelings. There is no need for placing of blame. There is no need to punish yourself. It helps a great deal to sort out the feelings and admit that they are there. Instead of playing, "what if," or "if only," it might help to say instead, "I am hurt," or "I am angry," or, "something happened to me and this is how I feel."

I have known people who sentenced themselves to years of suffering as payment for these feelings. One man who lost two children by drowning became an alcoholic because of the guilt he felt over not teaching his children to swim. For thirteen years he locked himself off from the world. He divorced his wife, would never speak of his children, never visited the cemetery and refused to deal with his feelings. He thought he deserved to suffer, and suffer he did.

Another woman became a hermit, a prisoner in her own home. She had unresolved feelings of guilt because she did not force her husband to go to the doctor when he showed signs of heart disease. She sentenced herself to loneliness to pay for her perceived failure.

I was asked to visit with a family after their young daughter-in-law was murdered. She and their son had just started college. The son came home one day to find that someone had broken into the apartment and murdered his wife. The boy's father said, "I am the one you need to talk to. I am so angry that, if I could find the guy who did this, I would kill him with my bare hands."

The mother said:

> I am not angry, I just feel guilty. I went with the kids when they were looking for an apartment. I found that apartment house and took them to see it. Now, if I had not found that apartment, they would not have been in that apartment, and the person would not have found her there. So, it is my fault.

I said, "Actually, you are just as angry as your husband, but you do not feel free to be angry at the person who did this terrible thing, so you have turned it inside and become angry at yourself."

I know others who spend the rest of their lives making the person who died into a saint. The loved one becomes larger than life; suddenly he or she becomes the perfect person. All the grieving person can talk about is how wonderful the deceased was when he/she was alive. Often this is a guilt reaction. It can be an effort to make up to the person for some slight, either real or imagined.

It is much healthier to deal with the feelings that you have. You are not to blame. You were not the perfect mate, father, mother, brother, sister, partner, or friend, but neither is anyone else. The road to understanding in grief is marked by finally reaching the realization that you were what you needed to be in this person's life, you made the wisest choices you could along the way, you did your best. Accept the fact that the "if onlys" block the gifts of memories that can sustain you.

*Grief is a family affair...*
*Healing rarely happens*
*off in lonely caves*
*away from*
*those we love.*

## Chapter 17

# It Takes a Family

The night before my grandmother's funeral, my father suggested that we go to the funeral home and visit with her. We sat beside her casket and began to tell stories about her life. We talked for a couple of hours and wished we could have stayed longer. I learned things about her that I did not know and was able to share some stories the family had never heard. I do not remember very much about her funeral the next day, but I never forgot that night and the stories.

I had no idea how valuable that night was until my father-in-law died a few years later. There was never an opportunity for us to gather as a family and tell stories. The coming and going of friends and families made it impossible to complete any stories we tried to share. I actually ached as I drove home. There were so many things I wanted to say and so many stories I wanted to hear; I realized there would never be a time when we would all be together at a time appropriate for story telling

When we got home my wife and I acted like nothing had happened. Her father's death became the elephant in the room no one would talk about. Families seem to build up barriers that will not allow them to talk about a death. I did not want to bring it up until I knew my wife wanted to talk about it and she was doing the same. I finally woke her up in the night and said, "I am missing your father." That broke through the barrier.

Seeing this happen in my family, and remembering how meaningful the story telling time for my grandmother was, led me to begin getting families together and helping them have a time for telling stories. It has become one of the things I enjoy and find most meaningful. And it has proven to be meaningful to families as well. A couple of years ago a man thanked me for a family story time I provided after his grandmother's death thirty-five years ago.

Not only does this break barriers, it actually keeps the person alive among the family. No one is dead until they are forgotten, and my grandmother is still alive to us. As long as her immediate family was alive they told those same stories every time they got together. I often said I not only knew the stories they would tell, I knew the order in which they would be told.

I now try to meet with grieving families together as a grief group unto themselves. I met regularly with a family whose nineteen-year-old son died of self-inflicted gunshot. I cannot express how important these meetings became. Each family member expressed where they were and what they were feeling which allowed the other members to understand that each person was grieving in a way that fit them. They did not show their grief in the same way or to the same intensity, but each one was in grief and they found ways to understand and accept the diversity of feelings.

One significant thing came out when I met with that family. I asked them how much they were talking to each other outside of the group meetings and they said they were not talking very much at all. They were saving it for the safety of the meetings. It is very hard for families to talk to each other. They seem to be afraid their emotions will get out of hand and they won't know how to get things back into control.

It makes me shudder to think of the families who do not have a safe place where they can dare talk. I recognize that this will be hard for a family to organize for themselves, but may I suggest that you try. Ask for a set time and place when the family will gather to simply tell stories to honor the loved one. Gathering for stories is not as threatening as gathering for grief counseling, so they may agree. This does not have to be a weekly meeting but it should be scheduled at least once per month.

This can be a way for a family to avoid hurting each other due to lack of communication or misinterpretation. If a parent dies, do the children give priority to the needs and feelings of the surviving parent, even if it means ignoring what their hearts are saying?

When a child dies, can the parents and siblings find common ground in how the memories are formed and how life goes on in the absence?

When a grandparent dies, do the grandchildren have a voice in the sharing or are they shunted to the side, without recognizing that the loss is great for them as well?

Set up a time to visit the graveside or columbarium, or just gather in a private setting and begin with a favorite memory. If you gather to tell stories, the sharing of grief will just happen naturally. Grief is a family affair. It impacts the whole family and it takes the whole family to work through the pain and find health. Healing rarely happens off in lonely caves away from those we love. It happens best in a circle of family sharing and supporting each other.

*Healing always begins
in the grieving
person's bucket.*

# Chapter 18
# Safe People

Most of the help we receive comes from our friends. Unfortunately, a lot of the hurt we receive will also come from our friends; friends who mean well and want to make us feel better, but end up trivializing our grief and trying to explain it away while trying to help.

I carry a couple of buckets with me everywhere I go when presenting a seminar. I ask someone from the audience to hold one of the buckets and explain that it represents the feelings one has after the loss of a loved one. The volunteer and the audience talk about what would be in the bucket. The main idea is to show how people are overflowing with feelings during grief. I then pick up my bucket and explain that it is full of platitudes and statements designed to make the person feel better and that I want to stand back and pour what is in my bucket into the one the person is holding. We agree that there is no room in the full bucket for anything I have to say.

I then ask, instead of my pouring my stuff into the already full bucket, what if I simply hugged the person and said, "That must really hurt"? It becomes very evident that a hug and that statement would really help. It meant I was getting in their bucket with them instead of standing off to the side throwing platitudes at an already overwhelmed heart and mind.

That exercise always reminds me of two very valuable truths. First, healing always begins in the grieving person's bucket. It never begins in my bucket. There is nothing in my bucket that will make the grieving person feel better.

The second truth is, "That must really hurt," is the most comforting thing we can say to a person in grief. That is counter to how people normally think, of course. The norm is to try to put the best face on the loss or fix it in some way. In the process they trivialize the pain and try to take away the grief. When someone says, "That must really hurt," they are legitimizing your pain and giving you permission to grieve. There are many ways to say it but the message is: "I am aware that this is a massive hurt in your life and I am comfortable enough to acknowledge it and walk with you through it."

People who do that become *safe* to you. Your grief demands that you have safe people and safe places where your grief is accepted and your grieving does not make them nervous or scared. There is no good explanation for why some folks feel safe and others do not. Somehow you will feel freer around certain people and, many times they will not be established friends or family. Safe people are rare indeed. If you are lucky enough to find one, stay close to him/her until the hardest part of the storm is passed and do so no matter how left out your old friends and family feel. These are the people who will crawl into your bucket and just listen.

I cannot stress enough how important it is that someone listens to you. Grief shared is grief reduced. We deal
with the anger and negative feelings by talking to safe
ears.

To say we work through our grief by talking to safe
ears sounds rather simplistic. There must be a more
definitive and active way of dealing with your feelings. It
may sound simple but there are some dynamics happening when you are listened to. As you talk you are ordering your mind. Talking and being heard gradually stops
the whirl and helps the mind begin to focus and see
through the maze of thoughts. Things begin to fit. Concepts begin to form and you can begin to understand
why you feel the way you feel.

On one of our trips to work with professional counselors in New York after September 11th, a woman told
her story to the group I was meeting with. She said the
person who helped her the most when her son died was
her friend. While every other friend was busy telling her
how she should feel, act and react, her friend would just
listen. She said:

> I would tell her how I felt and she would say, 'You know,
> you are absolutely right.' The next day I would con-
> tradict everything I said the day before and my friend
> would say, 'You know, you are absolutely right.' The
> next day I might contradict everything I said both days
> before and she would respond the same way. She simply
> listened while my mind ordered itself and figured out
> how to feel.

People get insights into problems when they are
heard. I often say I have no idea how counseling works.
I just sit with my chin in my hand and say a few words

every once in a while and somehow folks seem to get better. As they talk they are discovering realizations into how they feel and why they feel the way they do. People have the capability to heal themselves. The counselors are just the catalyst that allow people to find healing on their own path.

It sounds too easy and uncomplicated, but safe ears are the most powerful healing force there are for facing your grief.

*When a death happens we want someone to crawl into our bucket with us and simply try to understand what has happened to us.*

# Chapter 19

# Safe People Understand

The one thing you are looking for and the most healing thing anyone can do for you is wrapped up in the word understanding. People want to be understood. To have someone really listen and try to understand what you are feeling without trying to fix it or explain it away is healing; hard to find, treasured when found.

Four months after my wife died, my eyesight suddenly weakened until I had to give up driving a car. Living alone without transportation impacts more than we have time to discuss but, needless to say, independence and spontaneity are high on the list. I watched how people responded to my telling them about this loss. Almost without exception the first response was something like, "Well, now you know anytime you need a ride I am more than willing to drive you." Everyone wanted to help, but they thought help was offering to drive and eliminating the problem. That, of course, made me feel trivialized on the one hand and even less independent on the other. Every time I want to go somewhere I must bother some friend? The more people I told, the more rides I was offered, and the worse I felt.

Then my family responded with "This is a terrible burden and you must feel awful." Actually they said those words in more graphic language, but you get the idea. That not only felt wonderful, it felt like I had been understood, it did not seem to be nearly as big a problem, and I could stop talking about it and get busy finding ways to solve my transportation needs. Had they not done so I would still be looking for someone who would simply understand. We need folks who will understand first and then try to help us fix it.

I am not sure we can actually move past our pain until someone understands. A woman recently told her story to a college class. The class had just viewed a video about the power of being understood and that triggered her story. She was a paramedic in Oklahoma City the day the bomb blew up the Federal Building. She was due to get off duty after a long night when the call came and she and her team went to the scene and worked incredibly long hours in the horror of that scene. She said:

> I just figured out why I have not been able to put that experience behind me. I have been through post traumatic stress counseling and personal counseling and, so far, nothing has worked. As I watched the video it dawned on me that no one ever asked me how I felt. They asked me what I saw in great detail over and over. I ultimately divorced my husband because all he wanted was the gory inside story instead of understanding what his wife had experienced. My friends asked me what I said and what others said. But no one ever asked me what I felt.

No one understood and she was still looking, even though she did not know what she was looking for.

When bad things happen to us we have a tremendous need to tell our story. There are actually two sides to the story. First, we need to explain what we are experiencing, how we felt when our loved one died, what we have lost, what fears grip us. That is human nature. Turn on the television after a terrible storm has hit an area and listen to the reporter's interview the eye witnesses. There can be death and destruction everywhere, but the first thing the eye witnesses talk about is what they experienced and what they felt. They don't mean it, of course, but it sounds like they are saying, "You think those people have problems—let me tell you it almost scared me to death!"

When a death happens we want someone to crawl into our bucket with us and simply try to understand what has happened to us. They can't fully understand and no one will ever know exactly how we feel, but if they make the effort it is healing.

The other side of the story is to let the world know the value and impact of the loved one who has died. We want to tell the world what they meant to us and how valuable they were to others. We need someone to understand what has been lost and how much that loss will mean to our lives.

If our stories are heard and understood we can begin to move on. If not we tend to park and make very little, if any, progress. I do not use the idea of people getting stuck in their grief very much because too often friends and family think someone is stuck just three months after the death. Some people do get stuck. I am convinced that the ones who do so are the ones who were never understood.

*No one knows as much about grief as those who are walking through it.*

# Chapter 20

# How Do We Help Ourselves?

Grief recovery is not a passive experience. We don't just sit back and cry our way through the tough times and then wake up all better some bright morning. We have a role to play as well. I have made an effort to keep my own grief journey behind the scenes in this book. I did not want it to be about me. The truth is my wife died a few months before I began working on this book. I tried to keep as open minded as possible in order to observe what helped me in my journey. I do not present these as some kind of magic plan, or even as a path for you to follow. Nor do I claim any credit for the concepts listed here. Most of the ideas have come from observing others as they faced grief. I have noticed that some individuals seem to progress better than others. Most of that may be caused by the different relationships and losses. But at least some of it must have come from some tendencies I have noticed in those who seem to face their grief and deal with the emotions in a healthy way. Out of my experience and observations have come some suggestions I hope will resonate with you in a helpful way.

## Build A Support System

Support systems rarely just appear out of thin air. Most of your friends do not know what to say and are so afraid of saying the wrong thing that they are uncomfortable being around you or will avoid you all together. Others are just not comfortable talking about anything that relates to death. And some do not like to deal with emotions on any level. Most of us must build our own support system. When our hearts are broken the last thing we want or need is a job or a search, but passively waiting for saviors to come along is usually futile. I get e-mail responses from the grief blog I write and almost everyone starts off with "I have no one to talk to," or "My friends and family are tired of listening to me".

Building a support system can require that you recognize the need and take some positive actions. Almost every city of any size will have grief support groups. These are usually offered by hospices, hospitals, or church groups. Seek them out. They are time consuming and can be hard to take at times, but you will come closer to finding safe people there with whom you can form a friendship and become mutually supportive. No one knows as much about grief as those who are walking through it.

Sometimes we just have to train our friends. Pick out one or two you can trust will not be offended and give each a copy of a good book on grief. Tell him/her right up front that you are looking for a companion, not a counselor, and that they do not have to have answers. You just want to borrow their ears and wear them out.

You may just have to pull away from those who want to fix you and are full of advice and scriptures that are supposed to make you feel better but are really an effort to take your grief away from you.

## Don't Hide Your Bucket

This one is the one I needed to hear and the one I struggled with the most. I have always been the big healer and find it very hard to be the one in need of healing. I have been the one to bless others and frankly don't know how to let others bless me. When someone asked how I was, I could almost feel myself putting my bucket behind my back and saying, "I am fine," or, if I was trying not to be defensive saying, "I am doing as well as could be expected." Some of that comes from being a male and trying not to show any weakness, but most of it comes from a fear of intimacy. Men are not the only ones who hide their buckets. Women are just more subtle and smarter. All of us must learn how to let others into our innermost feelings.

Of course, you do have the right to choose who you let into your buckets. You cannot just let your guard down and share with anyone who asks. One of the questions I am often asked is, "How are we supposed to respond when someone asks how we are doing?" I think you have the right to respond however you feel like responding at that particular moment. If the person seems to be asking the question just because they think they are expected to, then you have the right to say "Fine," and walk on by. Even if the person is sincere and, at some other time or place you would love to share with them but do not feel like doing so at that time or in that place, you still have the right to say you are fine and wait for a better time and setting. You even have the right to say, "I would love to talk to you in depth sometime soon, but I am just not able to do so today. Thanks for asking," and move on.

When you can do so, pull the bucket from behind your back and let someone crawl in there with you.

## Give Yourself Permission To Get Well

There comes a time when you have to decide that it is all right to live again; that you can laugh without failing to properly mourn; that you can live without forgetting; that you can think of something else without failing to honor the relationship.

A dear friend of mine named Paula Loring, one of the very best grief companions I know, has a beautiful description of the grief process. She describes it as:

When the heart breaks
When the heart bleeds
When the heart surrenders
and
When the heart heals

I think the heart surrendering happens when we give ourselves permission to live again.

I have a dear friend whose fear of forgetting her son has caused her to maintain her grief for a very long time. If she begins to feel a little bit better, she reads his diary and falls apart all over again. She gets up to the point of surrender and backs away. She just can't seem to allow herself the permission to live again.

One of my favorite stories from the Bible concerns the man who lay by a pool that supposedly had healing properties. Once in a while the pool would bubble and, according to the legend at the time, the first person into the water would be healed. The man was carried there every day for several years of futility. He had no way to get into the water even if he had the chance to be first. In the story, the first thing Jesus asked him was, "Do you want to get well?" That was not a silly question, it was the determining question. The man was addicted to hopelessness and could not get well until he decided that he wanted to do so.

In a very real sense, you will at some point along the lonely road of your pain have to decide if you want to get well. Your answer will largely determine the outcome of your journey.

## Discover Gratitude

It seems to me that the people who find some way to be grateful handle their grief experience much better than others. The difference between those who learn to live again and those who spend years asking "why me" may well be a sense of gratitude. That was easy for me. The night my wife died I said, "I have had fifty-seven years of a wonderful marriage. All I can feel is grateful and lucky for a wonderful life." I will always feel that way and it made my long grief journey just a few steps shorter. The wonderful family whose nineteen-year-old son died of suicide said on more than one occasion that they were so glad they knew him and loved him for the brief years they had. Parents who must find a way to develop gratitude for a baby born too soon and discover memories of love that did not have a chance to grow; children who are thankful for lessons learned from a parent that will stay with them forever. It is that sense of gratitude which, I think, will make a profound difference on the long road ahead.

Gratitude to me is somehow connected to faith. Faith that says my life has been in the hands of someone outside of myself and I can trust that force to see me the rest of the way. In my experience, that is the knot that I can grab and hold on to at the end of my rope.

*I do not know any better way
to do this than by reaching out
to others in grief and becoming a
safe person to them
on their journey.
That is grief's
twelfth step.*

## Chapter 21
# Grief's Twelfth Step

His name was Tom. One of the best men I have ever known. He was a long time sober participant in Alcoholics Anonymous and he taught me much about life and how to recover from life's struggles. Even though he was well into his seventies and had been sober for so many years, he was always ready and willing to go try to rescue someone in need. I called him one time at 3:00 in the morning to go with me to get a young friend out of a bar and take him home. Watching Tom work with that young man was a marvel in understanding and love. When the young man was safely home, Tom and I had time to talk through the rest of the night. I asked him why he did this sort of thing and how he maintained his enthusiasm even at the ungodly hours when most rescue calls happened.

Tom's answer startled me. He said, "This is how I stay sober." He told me about the Twelfth Step of AA which demands that, when an alcoholic finds sobriety, he/she must then reach out to help others. That doing so actually helps keep them sober, not just because it is a reminder of what addiction can do to a life, but because it helps get them focused on something besides themselves. Addiction by its very nature means the person has become so self-absorbed that nothing matters except how they feel. Reaching out to others in the middle of the night demands that they think of others and, at least to that degree, breaks the hold of self-absorption.

After studying people all of my life I believe the most powerful and practical words ever spoken came from the mind of an itinerant carpenter's son. He said, "If you want to save your life, you must give it away." I think the closer we come to that concept the healthier we are emotionally as well as spiritually. The further we are from that concept the more mentally ill we become. If we are totally committed only to ourselves, we can commit crimes most people would cringe to even read about.

Grief demands that you turn inward and concentrate on your own healing. Self-absorption is almost a requirement, and is a healthy way to be during the struggle to survive. You must establish the depths of your loss and the value of the person you have lost. That requires you to concentrate on what is happening to your life. As you walk through the journey there comes a time when you need to begin to break the pattern of self-absorption and begin to get yourself off of your hands and no longer be dominated by how you feel. I do not know any better way to do this than by reaching out to others in grief and becoming a safe person to them on their journey. That is grief's twelfth step.

It is not hard to see the need for us to do so. Anyone in grief knows how hard it is to find safe people to talk with, and how to avoid those folks who hurt while trying to help. We can remember how lonely we were and how we longed for a warm body to listen to us without judgment or directions. Now that we know the need, we are uniquely equipped to be the one who gets out of bed in the middle of the night to sit with someone who can't see how they can possibly live over their pain. We know better than anyone how not to take grief away from another hurting heart.

The people I know who have done the best job of learning to live with their loved one's not being here are the ones who, in spite of their own pain, reached a shaky and still aching hand to someone who is just beginning this long and treacherous journey called grief.

Don't Take My Grief Away From Me

Notes

125

Don't Take My Grief Away From Me

## About the Author

# Doug Manning

Doug's career has included minister, counselor, business executive, author and publisher. He and his wife, Barbara, were parents to four daughters and long-term caregivers to three parents.

After thirty years in the ministry, Doug began a new career in 1982 and has devoted his time to writing, counseling and leading seminars in the areas of grief and elder care. His publishing company, In-Sight Books, Inc., specializes in books, video and audio productions specifically designed to help people face some of the toughest challenges of life.

Doug has a warm, conversational style in which he shares insights from his various experiences. Sitting down to read a book from Doug is like having a long conversation with a good friend.

**Care Community** Visit TheCareCommunity.com
**thecarecommunity.com** for Doug's blogs

# Selected Resources from In-Sight Books

**By Doug Manning**
 *Building Memories: Planning a Meaningful Funeral*
 *Journey of Grief* DVD
 *Lean On Me Gently: Helping the Grieving Child*
 *The Power of Presence: Helping People Help People*
  Book or DVD
 *Sacred Moments: A Minister Speaks About Funerals*
 *Special Care Series*
 *Thoughts for the Lonely Nights* book/journal or CD
 *Thoughts for the Grieving Christian* book/journal or CD
 In Spanish: *Grief Care Series* 2 CD set

**Other Resources from In-Sight Books**
 *I Know Someone Who Died* coloring book
  by Connie Manning
 *The Empty Chair: The Journey of Grief After Suicide*
  by Beryl Glover
 *Memories Too Few: A Letter to Parents About Pregnancy
  Loss* by Kathy Manning Burns
 *The Shattered Dimension: The Journey of Grief After
  Suicide* DVD by Beryl Glover
 *Comfort Cards* bereavement card collection


**For a complete catalog or ordering information contact:**
In-Sight Books, Inc.
800.658.9262 or 405.810.9501
OrdersAndInfo@InSightBooks.com
www.InsightBooks.com

*Funeral Homes may also order In-Sight Books products from
your Dodge Company representative or by calling The Dodge
Company at 800.443.6343*